AMAZING ANIMAL FRIENDSHIPS

ODD COUPLES IN NATURE

Written by Pavla Hanáčková

Illustrated by Linh Dao

SCRIBBLERS

a SALARIYA *imprint*

This edition published MMXVIII by Scribblers,
an imprint of The Salariya Book Company Ltd
25 Marlborough Place,
Brighton BN1 1UB

HB ISBN-13: 978-1-912006-48-9

1 3 5 7 9 8 6 4 2

SALARIYA
SCRIBO BOOK HOUSE SCRIBBLERS

© Designed by B4U Publishing, 2016
A member of Albatros Media Group
Author: Pavla Hanáčková
Illustrations: Linh Dao
www.b4upublishing.com
All rights reserved.
Translation rights arranged though JNJ Agency, Texas Allen
English text © The Salariya Book Company Ltd MMXVIII

A CIP catalogue record for this book is available
from the British Library.

Printed and bound in China.

Visit
www.salariya.com
for our online catalogue and
free fun stuff.

Table of contents

Pulling together..4

Zebras & oxpeckers 6

Hippos & fish 8

Bees & plants 10

Wrasses & large fish..12

Truffles & trees 14

Antelopes & baboons...16

Common clownfish & anemones...........................18

Ants & aphids...20

Pandas & bacteria..22

Hermit crabs, shells & anemones 24

Honey badgers & honeyguides..............................26

Sloths, algae & moths 28

Whale sharks & small fish.....................................30

Coyotes & American badgers................................32

Shrimps & gobies 34

Pulling together

Two is better than one - that's a fact! It's no surprise, therefore, that many plants and animals find a way to help each other. There are many examples of this on land, sea and even under the ground!

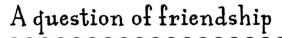

A helping hand

A question of friendship

Why do small birds often sit on zebras' backs? Is it possible for stinging anemones and fish to be good neighbours? And why don't sharks snack on the small fish swimming around them? It's because they have a **beneficial relationship** and help each other! ◄

A spot of help

For some creatures, such help is an advantage, but not a necessity. A hermit crab, for example, likes to place a roommate on its shell – an anemone! The anemone serves as a bodyguard to drive away any predators that might otherwise see the crab as "dinner". However, hermit crabs often do without the help of anemones. Such a relationship is called **symbiosis.** ▶

Wanna be friends?

Well...

Inseparable pair

By contrast, some partnerships are dependent on mutual assistance, like the relationship between plants and their pollinators. Without bees, beetles and various other insects, plants would not even be able to grow! This type of relationship is vital. It is called **mutualism.** ▾

We're the best of friends!

Pollinators & plants

Friendship aside

Not all creatures have a two-way relationship, quite the contrary; ticks and mosquitoes, for instance, do nothing for the host animal they land on. The host is simply a food source. ▾

Show me, honeyguide, where to find honey!

A friend in need is a friend indeed

It's good to have a reliable partner. Cooperating is advantageous because it makes it easier to find food, or be alerted to enemies. People recognise this logic, too – for instance, honey gatherers in Africa are accompanied by a honeyguide, a small bird that guides them to the honey. This kind of relationship is called **cooperation.** ◂

5

Zebras & oxpeckers

Animal dermatologist

In the African savannas, you will find various kinds of large mammals grazing on the grass. There is no lack of predators which makes it necessary for most animals to be on their guard. In order to escape danger, they need to be alert and able to run very, very fast. That's why, in a moment of peace, they certainly appreciate being pampered and licked into shape.

Oxpecker

People go to their doctor if they have skin problems. Animals in the African savannas have their doctor, too – and he's very much in demand! He's none other than a little bird called the **oxpecker**. ▾

OXPECKER'S
beauty & wellness salon

Common zebra

Whenever these striped zebras want to look their best, they employ the services of oxpeckers. These little birds peck out all the troublesome insects from their fur. This service is of advantage to them both, as the pecked-out lice make a delicious snack! ▶

Oxpecker's beak

Handy beauty salon

The oxpecker's distinctive beak is a great tool to groom many kinds of animal fur. They use it to quickly comb and clean the fur. They always stay close to animal herds, and are therefore at their clients' disposal at all times. ◀

Wily oxpecker

Watch out, though! Don't let the oxpecker's cute appearance fool you! If a zebra has an open wound, the oxpecker enjoys poking at it with its sharp beak for the taste of blood. It can even forage deep into the zebra's ear to reach earwax and ticks! ▶

A thorough examination

It's well worth the wait!

Diverse clientele

It's not only zebras that appreciate the oxpecker for its services – its clientele includes **giraffes, buffalos, rhinos** and **hippos**, too. All of them stand totally still so they don't disturb the oxpecker while it's working. What perfect patients! ▼

Next, please!

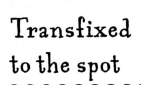

Transfixed to the spot

The oxpecker's strong legs help to keep it attached to the animal's hide as they groom. They can even stay attached to a hippo's slippery skin! ▶

Hippos & fish

Underwater washing service

Hippos spend a lot of time each day wallowing in water, only rarely coming to shore. They leave the water at night to graze. In the course of a day, many uninvited guests can easily attach themselves to their skin. Hippos are generally surrounded by many helpers that provide them with a complete cleaning service.

Taxi...!

From time to time, hippos become a taxi service. While moving in the water they transport various animals, like **herons** or **turtles** that hitch a ride. Why exert yourself needlessly, when hippos are so obliging? ▼

I'd like to go that way, please...

Hippopotamus

Hippos are no lightweights (they can weigh up to three tons), but they're great swimmers and are even capable of running along the riverbed, or remaining underwater for as long as ten minutes. Baby hippos love swimming lessons! ▼

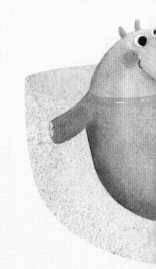

A full service?

Fish dentists

Fish are so thorough in their work that they don't even forget the hippo's mouth. They swim right in between its huge teeth, cleaning its tongue and the inside of its enormous mouth. ◄

Belly full of goodies

Clean as a whistle!

Because hippos are herbivores, they eat only plants. However, these can sometimes be hard to digest. Special microbes live inside the hippo's stomach, and these little helpers make it easier to digest even very coarse and stringy foods. ▲

Fishy vacuum cleaners

A **carp-like fish** uses its fleshy lips to attach itself to a hippo's skin to remove algae, parasites and dead skin cells one by one. There are other kinds of species that look after some less accessible spots, too.
▶

Wait! We haven't finished...

Uninvited passenger

Hippos often have other rather unwelcome passengers on their bodies – blood-sucking **leeches** that exclusively target hippos. ▶

A free lunch AND ride, awesome!

Bees & plants

Nectar drinkers

There's nothing more enticing than a colourful garden with its intoxicating scents wafting in the air and the soft hum of bees buzzing from flower to flower. Plants and pollinators belong with each other and can't survive apart. Pollinators carry pollen from one plant to another to pollinate them. The pollinators collect pollen or nectar in return.

The process of pollination

Diligent pollinators

Plants can't go off in search of another plant to reproduce, so they need the help of pollinators. The aim is to get pollen particles from one plant to another, whether by the help of water, wind or animal. Some plants, however, are capable of pollinating themselves. ◄

Move over... it's my turn!

Sweet nothings

Plants, too, need to attract pollinators. Bees like colourful blooms with a sweetish scent and a good landing area. Ladybirds usually search for large open blossoms with strong stalks. ►

Choosing the right flower

Insect pollinators

Amongst the ranks of industrious insect workers are various kinds of **beetles, moths** and **flies.** Flies lay their eggs into the body of a decomposing animal. This is why they are easily fooled by flowers smelling like rotten meat. When they lay their eggs into blooms, they carry the pollen with them to other plants. ▶

Four-legged pollinators

The Australian marsupial **honey possum** sucks nectar from blossoms and is one of the best known mammal pollinators. The **black-and-white ruffed lemur**, one of the lemurs living in Madagascar, is by far the largest pollinator there. ◀

Bird pollinators

Birds, too, pollinate flowers, especially those blooms that are large, colourful and with a sufficient supply of nectar. Such pollinators include **hummingbirds, honeyeaters** and **flowerpeckers.** They have a long thin beak which enables them to reach deep into the flowers and suck the nectar right out of it while staying in the air and rapidly flapping their wings. ▼

Mmm... It's SO yummy!

Bat specialists

Bats also help with this pollinating business, especially in tropical regions. Banana and mango trees are completely dependent on bats in order to be able to produce fruit. Bats have elongated snouts and their tongues can be up to eight centimetres long. As they gorge on the fruit their snouts get covered in pollen which then gets carried to other plants. ▶

Mangos for lunch!

Bat pollination

Wrasses & large fish

Cleaning station

Even though fish live in water, they still need a wash and brush up! They don't need any soap though - just a bunch of cleaners! All they have to do is swim by a cleaning station, get in line, and wait their turn. Little fish soon take charge of them, cleaning parasites from the surface of their body, gills, and oral cavity. About 45 species of fish and many shrimps provide this cleaning service.

Wrasses

Wrasses run their cleaning stations in coral reefs around the world's seas and oceans. There's no shortage of clients as wrasses are indispensable in this regard. They remove not only parasites and bacteria from their customers' skin, but also damaged or dead skin cells. ▶

Cleaning station

Competitors

Competition is stiff, so the cleaners have to know how to best attract customers. **Wrasses** rely on their striking colouration to instantly catch the attention of potential clients. They also move their body so that the sunlight will reflect on it. **Shrimps,** meanwhile, wave their claws and sometimes even add showy dance moves! ▶

Wait your turn, please

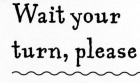

There are long queues, but all the customers wait in an orderly fashion – except for one predator. The **Barracuda** is attended to as a matter of priority and never has to wait. There are no objections as none of the queue wants to end up as a convenient snack! ◀

Barracudas don't queue!

Shrimps – cleaning specialists

If there's any place that the fish's tiny mouths can't reach, **shrimps** come to the rescue. Their long legs and claws provide an excellent tool. Shrimps use them to cut away pieces of protruding skin, or to pick leftover food from teeth. ▲

Fish pedicure

People decided to employ these services, too. Little fish quickly and efficiently remove dead skin from people's feet. ▶

Advantageous for both sides

So, why is this process mutually beneficial? Well, the fish end up amazingly clean, while the cleaners have a welcome feast. Even sharks, rays, cephalopods, and turtles enjoy this good service.

Truffles & trees

Underground friends

There are various kinds of mushrooms growing in the forests. Mushrooms, or fungi, are everywhere in nature, and can be found even under the ground. When you're walking around a forest, you're practically treading on them with every step. These fungi are fibres which grow through the soil, creating mycelium. There's a strong bond between fungi and tree roots which benefits both organisms.

Mushroom delicacy

Truffles are the diamond of all mushrooms. They can be divided into several types. Restaurants most often use **black** or **white truffles.** White truffles are the most expensive! They are even sold in auctions. The bigger the truffle, the more expensive it is. The price can reach well over one million dollars! ▶

White truffles

Black truffles

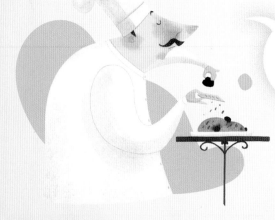

Oh-la-la! A freshly sliced truffle...

Truffles

Truffles are **fungi** which live alongside the roots of many trees. They grow under the ground where sows or specially trained dogs sniff them out by their strange smell. Truffles are considered a delicacy, sought after by gourmets around the world. ▲

Under the ground

The life-giving roots of plants are largely invisible as they are under the ground. These roots and various types of fungi make strong allies. Green plants provide fungi with nutrients gained from photosynthesis, while the fungi supply them with minerals and water. ▶

Clues for mushroom pickers

Every good mushroom picker knows which trees to look for. It's because some kinds of mushroom are dependent on particular trees, and are therefore found nearby. Truffles, for instance, do well near oaks. ▲

Invisible communication network

Mycelium and **tree roots** are connected and share warning signals about harmful substances. They use the same network of communication to share nutrients. ▶

Anything harmful about?

Nope! I'm doing great!

Wood-destroying fungi

Some kinds of mushrooms are of no benefit to trees, though. Quite on the contrary, they harm them by taking resources away! These are called **parasites** and include, for example, polypores. ◀

Antelopes & baboons

A watchful duo

While the antelopes calmly graze, baboons sit all around them. Suddenly, the animals grow restless. A predator? The savanna is teeming with lions, hyenas and leopards, so it's vital not to be caught unawares. Antelopes and baboons, however, have figured out a smart system - they live together because it doubles their chances of surviving dangerous predators.

Impala

What just flashed past? It was an impala, a slim, fast antelope that runs and leaps so quickly that it looks as though it's flying. When there's no danger lurking, an antelope likes being in the company of its herd. ▲

Animal superpowers

Antelopes and baboons make a good team. Antelopes have great hearing and can rotate their long ears in all directions, while baboons keep a very close watch on the surroundings. The more eyes there are, the more they see, which is why monkeys stick together in a pack. ▼

The coast's clear.

Baboon

When the night falls, baboon packs find shelter in tree tops. However, they spend their days on the ground, searching for food and improving on their relationships with other monkeys – by cleaning each other's fur or touching noses. ▶

You're my best friend ever...

People benefit, too

Humans soon realised that animals could offer them protection from danger. **People** have bonded with **dogs** since prehistoric times. One bark from a dog is enough to let us know something isn't right. ▲

I want to be alone!

Tell-tale expressions

Beware, danger!

No problem - relax!

Ha! I can see you...

Animal communication

Hunted by the same predators, baboons and antelopes have well established ways of interacting to warn each other of approaching danger. They communicate by various sounds, smells or postures as well as the baboon's facial expressions. ▲

Timely warning

Zebras and **ostriches** use a similar system. Contrary to their reputation, ostriches don't bury their head in the sand whenever danger is lurking! They have excellent eyesight and with their long necks can see far and wide. This makes it easy for them to spot lions creeping up on them through the high grass. Ostriches can't fly but they can run pretty fast (43 mph)! ▲

Common clownfish & anemones

Landlord and lodger

There are some very unlikely couples living in the ocean waters. Honestly! Surely nothing would voluntarily live next to a stinging anemone? However, common clownfish and small shrimps have figured out a way to adapt to such a life. Their neighbourly anemone won't sting them and, as a bonus, they're safe from dangerous predators!

Kids, I've got you a clown for your party!

Common clownfish

This brightly striped fish can be found near coral reefs and anemones. Anemones and clownfish can develop a **symbiotic relationship** which is beneficial to both of them. If a clownfish encounters danger without the protection of the anemone, it quickly swims back to its safe shelter. ◄

Stinging anemone

Anemones look like beautiful fragile flowers, but the opposite is true – they are predatory animals. Their tentacles have many **stinging cells** that they use to catch prey. The tentacles are covered with slime so that they don't sting each other. ▼

HOME SWEET HOME

Need help?

Other lodgers

Another of the anemones' lodgers includes **shrimps.** They, too, are immune to its stinging cells. They gradually develop immunity by rubbing against the tentacles and eating the slime. Once both organisms become acquainted, they help one another. ▲

Advantages of cohabitation

This co-existence offers many advantages to the shrimps. They are protected from predators and get food by cleaning the anemone, which in the process becomes wonderfully clean. Some shrimps even use the anemone as a place to provide their fish customers with cleaning services! ▶

When did you move in?

Adapted to cohabitation

Once the clownfish have a protective layer of slime on their bodies, there's nothing standing in the way of a good relationship. The anemone protects the fish, and they, in turn, take care of it by removing all dirt and by providing food. Their constant movement also brings oxygenated water to the anemone. ◀

Friends for life

Family house

Each pair of adult clownfish has its own house – an **anemone**. However, the couple needs to first get acquainted with the anemone, by rubbing their bodies against its tentacles in order to acquire some of the protective slime. The anemone offers protection only to its lodgers. It will sting any fish it doesn't know. ◀

Ants & aphids

Smart breeders

Ants are certainly hard workers. But where do they get all the energy to do such a lot of work? Next time you see an outdoor plant that looks slightly wilted, look underneath its leaves. You might see lots of small black or green bugs - aphids! This is what gives ants the energy to work tirelessly.

Diligent ants

An ant force divides its labour so that it can get as much done as possible. They're also extraordinarily strong, carrying burdens which are often much heavier than they are! ◄

Piece of cake, huh?

Weightlifters

Yummy!

Foodies

The discharged, thick nectar juice is called **honeydew** and ants like to feast on it. Honeydew makes up almost half their diet! All the ants need to do is tap an aphid on its bottom with their feeler, and the sweet delicacy is suddenly there. ▲

Sweet aphids

Aphids attack plants and suck out the sweet nectar, making the plant weak and wilting. There's so much nectar that the **aphids** are unable to eat it all and release the excess from their bodies. No wonder ants are always on the lookout for such walking 'goodies'! ►

Ant caregivers

Ants carry the aphids from place to place to find the best food for them – in order to ensure their stable supply of delicious nectar. Some ant species even take care of **aphid eggs**, the aphid babies, during the winter. ▼

Ant babysitting service

Personal bodyguard

Ants are always ready to protect aphids from danger or enemies who might want to enjoy them for dinner. ▶

I'll deal with this...

Spotted danger

A ladybird looks like a cute beetle, but it can quickly transform into a real predator. It hunts aphids and loves to eat them. Ants, however, don't like to be parted from their aphid friends... ▼

Termite mushroom pickers

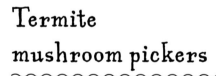

Some types of tropical ants grow their own **mushrooms** in their underground termite nests. These are their main source of food so they take excellent care of the mushrooms. Just take a look! ▼

Run! We'll hold him back.

Pandas & bacteria

Satisfied eaters

These adorable black-and-white pandas live happily among bamboo shoots, savouring its green leaves. But pandas devote so much time to eating that they need some assistance to digest it. Even though the assistants are really tiny and are never seen, they help pandas enormously.

Giant panda

Pandas, one of the most endangered species in the world, are bears that live in China. People try to protect, nurture and understand them as much as possible. Pandas are very different from common bears! ◄

Panda's "thumb"

Food, food and more food...

One of the things that makes the panda's all-day feasting easier is its paw. The panda has developed a **sixth finger**, similar to a thumb, which enables it to get a better grip on the bamboo stalk. ◄

Friendly bacteria

The panda's digestive system isn't designed for a plant-based diet, so various **friendly bacteria** help the bear to digest all that bamboo. These tiny assistants help the panda to break down at least some of the food it has consumed. ►

I'm full!

Ah... time for a snack.

Lazier than a sloth

Because the panda's diet isn't exactly rich in nutrients, they have learned to save as much energy as possible. There are two ways to do this – they sleep for more than half of the day, and eat for the rest of the time. If they need to move, they go very, very slowly. Even a sloth could outrun them! ▲

An untypical bear

A typical bear eats both meat and plants. Yet pandas almost exclusively eat bamboo. They can polish off up to twelve kilograms (26.5 lbs.) of **bamboo** a day! It's interesting that even though they've been eating bamboo for millions of years, their digestive tracts are the same as those of the other bears. ▼

Not only pandas

Pandas aren't the only ones who have bacteria in their stomach to help with digestion. Cows, horses, sheep, even giraffes have a similar arrangement! ▲

Panda's diet

Bear's diet

Hermit crabs, shells & anemones

Bodyguard on board

The small hermit crab makes its way confidently along the seabed. Attached to the shell on its back is an anemone that gently sways with the movement of the current. Whenever a predator approaches them, it gets stung by the anemone and turns tail. But how did the anemone end up on top of the shell?

Hermit crab without shell

Hermit crab

These crabs have a soft, vulnerable body that needs protection. That's why they search for abandoned **carapaces** or **shells** to use for this purpose. They climb into it and carry the new dwelling around on their back! It works perfectly, like a suit of armour. ◀

Always together

Crabs had an even better idea for protecting themselves from dangerous predators. They simply put an **anemone** onto their shell. It becomes their personal bodyguard. Any predator that approaches will pay the price. ▶

And don't come back!

Anemone

There are many anemone species living in the seas. Some are huge, but others are no bigger than a thumb. All of them have one thing in common, though – they sting, and touching them is very painful! ▲

A two-way bonus

You do the food, I take care of us

Why do anemones agree to this arrangement? It's because protecting the crab yields a particular reward for it: easy food. The anemone gets all the crab's leftover food to eat. ▲

A new home?

As the hermit crab grows bigger, it will need a larger dwelling. All it needs to do is find another, bigger abandoned shell to become its new home, and the crab simply moves to its new address. However, the bodyguard also needs to be moved. The crab uses its claws to gently transfer the anemone to the new shell so that they can continue living happily together. ▶

Which one to choose?

It's the latest fashion!

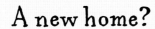

Improvisation

Hermit crabs can be kept in aquariums. They are very adaptable – if there are no shells around, they make do with a piece of wood, a stone, or some coral instead. They will even improvise and use man-made objects, like building blocks, as a shell. ◀

Honey badgers
& honeyguides

A smart pair

Both of these animals have 'honey' in their names because honey is their favourite snack. But, as it is not exactly the easiest food to reach, they have joined forces to locate it. By working together they have struck up a smart partnership to ensure that they are never short of honey.

Honey badger

The honey badger is an African predator that looks like a weasel or badger, only bigger. But don't let the honey badger's pleasant appearance fool you! It's fearless and will attack much larger animals than itself. ◄

Honeyguide

This tiny African bird is quite cunning. It's one of the few birds that feasts on bee larvae and even on beeswax. However, the honeyguide can't reach it on its own due to its short beak. So it has found a great solution! ▶

Daredevil and a powerhouse

The other half of this team, the **honey badger**, is the most fearless creature in the entire animal kingdom. It will attack almost anything – even a pack of lions! ▶

Run... you big pussy cat!

Brains and power

Both of these honey-lovers have their different strengths which they rely on to get to their favourite snack. The honey badger is very strong and copes with all the hard work, while the honeyguide is the brains behind the operation as it leads the honey badger to the location of the bee hive. ▶

The world's most fearless creature

Thick-skinned

The honey badger isn't at all worried about the angry bees stinging it. It is so well equipped for fighting, you see – it has tough skin which acts like armour, sharp claws, and strong jaws. ◀

Oh no, it's that guy again!

Search party in action

The honeyguide navigates and leads the honey badger to the destination by shrieking sharply and wagging its tail. Once they get to the hive, the honey badger uses its long sharp claws to tear it open so that both of them can enjoy the bee **larvae** and **beeswax**. ▶

Sloths, algae & moths

Camouflage in treetops

You need to really pay attention if you want to spot a sloth in its natural environment. Living its slow life in the treetops, it is very well camouflaged and almost indistinguishable from the surrounding greens.

I think this colour suits me!

Three-toed sloth

High-rise homes

Sloths are typically arboreal animals who spend most of their days hanging from tree branches. They have strong claws which prevent them from falling off. Occasionally they climb down to the ground, but don't stay there for long before climbing back up again. ◀

Smart disguise

A sloth moves so slowly that its fur gets covered with **algae**, which turns it a grey-green. It becomes like an invisibility cloak amongst the surrounding mass of green leaves! ▶

Master of disguise

I hang about here most days.

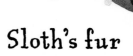

Sloth's fur

A sloth's body is adapted to hanging. Even its long fur grows in the opposite direction to most other animals. This makes it easier for rainwater to trickle downwards off the fur. ▲

Moth living in sloth's fur

Neighbours

The algae in a sloth's fur live on its sweat and on flakes of skin. But something else is lurking amongst all that hair, too! The sloth's fur is home to a **small moth** which doesn't mind sharing. ▲

Hmm? Nothing for lunch here!

In treetops

Sloths live in the treetops and only crawl down when they need to urinate. Once their paws touch the ground, the sloths become incredibly vulnerable because moving on ground is very hard for them. They seem to crawl rather than walk, which makes them easy prey for jaguars or harpy eagles. ▶

Slow, slow and slower

Sloths are very slow and move with no sense of hurry. Even their **digestion** is slow. They only have to go down to answer the call of nature once every 2-4 weeks! The advantage of this, however, is safety. By not moving, the sloth isn't seen by its enemies. ◀

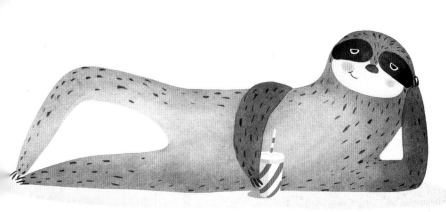

Whale sharks & small fish

Fish bodyguard

There's a great variety of creatures living in the sea - some of them are tiny, others huge, and often they co-exist happily together! Curiously, it's not always the case that a larger animal will automatically want to eat smaller ones. Often this strange 'little and large' relationship works perfectly.

Sharks

Sharks are amongst the most feared sea predators. A shark looks like a torpedo with a huge tail fin. Once a **shark** stops swimming, it also stops breathing, and eventually drowns. That's why it always keeps moving, along with its buddy, the sharksucker, attached to its body. In this way, the sharksucker travels the length and breadth of the ocean. ▲

Hi there...

Special sucker

Suckers

Sharksuckers remain attached to these huge creatures by clinging to them with a special sucker. They use it to latch onto their host and stay put. ◄

Handy little helpers

Good morning
Mr. Shark!

Protection and diet

Sharksuckers remove impurities from the body of their host and take care of its health. In return for this service, sharks and other hosts give them protection, and sometimes even food when they drop something tasty while eating. ▲

New buddy

No sharks or rays at hand? Never mind, the sharksucker is not fussy! It doesn't turn up its nose at anything – not even a **diver**. All sharksuckers need is a bit of bare skin to latch onto. Even the diver's forehead will do! ▼

Sea predators

Sharksuckers attach themselves to other huge beasts, too, such as **whales, rays, turtles**, or **mantas**. ▲

Big fish: small fish

Some sea giants are surrounded by numerous shoals of small fish. The tiny fish don't fear these huge creatures because they won't hurt them. The small fish take care of these creatures and are rewarded with food and a 'lift'. ◄

Coyotes & American badgers

Hunters

Two particular beasts of prey on the American prairies make up a very unexpected but successful pair of hunters. The coyote and the badger, when paired together, form a deadly hunting duo that relentlessly pursue their prey.

Coyote

Coyotes hunt at dusk in small packs or, sometimes, alone. They can be sure their prey won't escape them because they are good runners – the fastest of all wild dogs! Given the opportunity, coyotes love to feast on small rodents that tend to hide away in underground holes. ◄

Missed again!

American badger

The badger is a predator with a taste for small rodents. It's a great digger with **strong claws** that can dig faster than a man with a shovel. ▼

Let me tell you something about coyotes...

Great digger

Even smarter!

The Coyote holds a special place in Native American mythology and features in numerous stories where it's described as a resourceful and smart creature. And it's true! Coyotes have figured out a system which is greatly beneficial to them. ►

Prairie dog

The **prairie dog** is not a dog but a small rodent that lives in underground holes along with its large extended family. Those underground tunnels are interconnected to form entire cities. The prairie dogs build up the banks around the exit which serve as look-out towers. They often stand, bolt upright, to scan their surroundings for signs of danger. ◄

Thanks, partner!

A well-coordinated team

Partnership

The coyote's excellent sense of smell allows it to track its prey. On the other hand, the badger is equipped with very strong front paws that help it to drive prey out of holes. And so they came together and figured – hey, why don't we try working as a team? And so, the lethal hunting couple was born. The coyote doesn't eat the badger because they make such a good team together! ►

Strength in a pack

These two sly hunters aren't the only ones to recognise that there's strength in numbers. Other predators, for example lions or wolves, hunt in a similar way, but in **packs**, with great success. ◄

Shrimps & gobies

Underwater excavator and look-out

Who's that working so hard on the seabed? Ah - it's a shrimp. It keeps running into a tunnel and back out again carrying sand in its claw each time. A fish swimming nearby never moves too far away. This unlikely couple forms another team that also works well together.

Pistol shrimp

Underwater tunneller

These small pistol shrimps spend their entire day digging and taking care of their hole. One of the **shrimp's claws** is noticeably bigger than the other and can make a sound similar to a gunshot. This is how shrimps hunt their food – they stun their victims with this loud noise. Even though shrimps look tough, they're almost completely blind and need protection. ◄

Shared household

The shrimp shares its **tunnel** with the goby fish. Because they want to keep their home nice and clean, the shrimp diligently cleans it by regularly carrying out armfuls of sand. ►

We like our house nice and clean.

All clear!

Sharp-sighted watchman

Why does the shrimp share his tunnel with a goby? The fish has sharp eyesight that provides protection for the shrimp and is always on the lookout for any approaching danger. ◄

Danger approaching

Whenever something even remotely suspicious occurs near their house, the fish and shrimp send each other a special **signal** which means only one thing: take cover! Both buddies quickly hide in their hole. As soon as the danger passes, the fish swims out to check that all is safe again. Only then does the shrimp emerge. ◄

Helping hand

The fish is in constant contact with the shrimp even though the shrimp is always running back and forth. You see, the shrimp touches the fish with its **feelers** at all times. That is the way they communicate. ►

Other advantages

And what does the fish get in return for his protection service? Apart from sharing his cosy beautiful home, the shrimp also shares food with the little fish, who gets to eat all the shrimp's leftovers! ◄

Algae Plantlike organisms that live mainly in water and use the energy from the Sun to produce food and survive.

Arboreal Types of animal that live in trees.

Bamboo Types of large, treelike grass found mainly in East and Southeast Asia.

Carapace The hard upper shell of species such as the tortoise, crab and lobster.

Cephalopod A type of marine animal that includes octopus, squid and cuttlefish.

Dermatologist A medical specialist who can treat skin conditions.

Mycelium The branching, tube-shaped parts of a fungus that produce spores which allow the fungus to reproduce.

Nectar A sugary liquid produced by plants to attract insects and other animals.

Prairies A type of grassland, found mainly in North America.

Index & Glossary

A
algae 9, 28–29
anemone 4, 18–19, 24–25
antelope 16–17
aphid 20–21

B
baboons 16–17
bacteria 12, 22–23
badger
 American 32–33
 honey 26–27
bat 11
bees 5, 10–11, 26–27

C
clownfish 18–19
coyote 32–33

G
gobies 34–35

H
hermit crab 4, 24–25
hippopotamus 7–9
honeyguide 5, 26–27

L
ladybird 10, 21
leech 9

M
monkeys 16
moth 11, 28–29

O
ostrich 17
oxpecker 6–7

P
panda 22–23
prairie dog 33

S
shark 4, 13, 30–31
sharksucker 30–31
shrimp 12–13, 18–19, 34–35
sloth 23, 28–29

T
trees 11, 14–16, 28–29
truffles 14–15
turtle 8, 13, 31

W
whale shark 30–31
wrasses 12–13

Z
zebra 4, 6–7, 17